Life to the Full

LORETTA ANDREWS

D0234275

WORD PUBLISHING

WORD ENTERTAINMENT LTD
Milton Keynes, England

LIFE TO THE FULL

First published 2001 by Word Publishing,
9 Holdom Avenue, Bletchley,
Milton Keynes, Bucks, MK1 1QR, UK

1-86024-215-4

All biblical quotations are from The Youth
Bible, New Century Version (Anglicised
Edition) © 1993 by Thomas Nelson, Inc.

Design and layout by Giles Davies.
Cover and text illustrations by David Fenton.

Produced for Word Publishing by
Christian Publicity Organisation,
Worthing, BN13 1BW, England.
Printed in Great Britain

THANKS

Special thanks to everyone who has helped to make this book happen: Malcolm Down and everyone at Word Publishing, John and Sue Ritter, Mark and Gareth, and everyone at Alliance. Thanks to Giles Davies for the wonderful design and David Fenton for the brilliant illustrations and cover.

Thanks and big hugs to all my guinea pigs who contributed and let me test it out on them - the other Shine girlies Han, Nic and Tash, Claire Hendy from Leon School, Lucy Quist and Abbey Cunningham who are members of a local church youth group, and David Fenton.

This book is dedicated to all the pupils Shine have met in the Milton Keynes Secondary Schools.

Contents

About Shine

Shine are an all-girl Pop/R&B group who work predominantly in the secondary schools of Milton Keynes and its surrounding areas under the Shine Trust.

Shine present the Christian message to teenagers in a relevant and exciting way by taking RE lessons, assemblies and performing concerts at schools and taking music, dance and drama lessons. They tour all over Europe when they are not in schools. Shine have recorded two albums which are available from most Christian bookshops.

Name: **Loretta Andrews**
Became a Christian: **Age 14**
Fave Bible Verse: **Proverbs 16:3.**
'Depend on the Lord in whatever you do, and your plans will succeed.'

Name: **Hanne Pettersen**
Became a Christian: **Age 9**
Fave Bible Verse: **Psalm 37:4-5.**
'Enjoy serving the Lord, and he will give you what you want. Depend on the Lord; trust him, and he will take care of you.'

Name: **Natasha Andrews**
Became a Christian: **Age 14**
Fave Bible Verse: **Ephesians 3:18.**
'And I pray that you and all God's holy people will have the power to understand the greatness of Christ's love - how wide and how long and how high and how deep that love is.'

Name: **Nicola Rodgers**
Became a Christian: **Age 11**
Fave Bible Verse: **Psalm 91:1-2.**
'Those who go to God Most High for safety will be protected by the Almighty. I will say to the Lord, "You are my place of safety and protection. You are my God and I trust you".'

Preface

I did not grow up in a Christian family, but I became a Christian at the age of 14. I had never really believed that we just live, die and that's it! So, the first time I heard about how much God loves me, what Jesus has done for me and how I could get in on 'Life to the full' I just knew it was the truth and knew I didn't want to miss out on it. I thought to myself: 'How do I know if this works?' Well, how do you know anything works? - By trying it! So I did, and in the last ten years God has proved himself to be real to me time and time again. But what a journey it's been. Don't let anyone tell you it's easy being a Christian (in fact Jesus said the opposite), but it is also the most fulfilling life there is and, frankly, anything else seems like second best in comparison.

anything else seems like 2nd best in comparison

The morning after I became a Christian I remember having a bit of a panic attack and thinking 'Oh no, what if I've done the wrong thing by becoming a Christian - is this what I really want?' All sorts of other doubts and fears came into my head. I knew I'd made a hugely significant decision that would affect my whole life and, to be honest, it was pretty scary. But then I thought to myself: 'If this stuff is really true then of course I want it', so I decided then and there to stick at it.

However, I still felt more than a little overwhelmed and lost, and wondered how to start living this new life ahead of me on a daily basis? I had all sorts of questions that I was too scared to ask, and felt guilty for having doubts too. I have since found out that what I was feeling was perfectly understandable and normal for a 'baby Christian' (as I was) - but I didn't realise that at the time. Therefore, it has always been my ambition to write a book like this and dedicate it to all young people out there who have either just made that decision or are thinking it through and are feeling exactly the way that I did. Hey, you're normal! It's OK to have doubts, and it's OK to have questions - there are answers - it's all part of growing up into this new and amazing adventure called 'life with God.' So I hope this helps you.

Loretta

r e l a t i o n

Introduction

As part of one of our lessons in the Milton Keynes schools, we conducted a little survey to find out what things are important in the lives of young people. We asked three questions - perhaps you'd like to think about them yourself:

❶ What is your most precious possession?

❷ What is your happiest moment?

❸ What is your biggest ambition?

A recent survey showed that most people believe that, in order to be happy and fulfilled, they need to have one or more of the following: MONEY, FREEDOM, RELATIONSHIPS, CAREER, POPULARITY, & LOOKS. Amazingly, in each class, every answer given fitted into one or more of these six categories. I'm sure you will find the same with your answers. For example, if your most precious possession is your mum, that comes under relationships, or if your happiest moment was when you did a bungee jump that would come under freedom and if your biggest ambition is to play for Manchester United, that could come under money, career and popularity.

However, if all our happiness and fulfilment is based *only* on these six categories we are faced with a problem. Take a closer look at the six categories. OK, so there is nothing wrong with wanting any of these things - indeed most of us would admit to being happier with some or all of them - *but*, all of these things can come to an end, breakdown, run out or fail you. So what then? What becomes of our happiness and fulfilment in life?

Ask yourself this: what if there is something we can have in our lives that gives us lasting fulfilment and deep happiness that can't be destroyed or taken away from us and that will never fail us or let us down?

Sounds *too good to be true* doesn't it? Well, what if I told you *that* **there really is something**, any one can have it and, furthermore, it's free! So what is it? How do I get it? And how do I make the most of it?

Interested?

Then read on . . .

Real fulfilment and lasting happiness that never leave you or fail you can only be found through having God involved in your life and having a friendship with him. What do I mean by a friendship with God? Well, to understand that fully we have to go right back to the beginning where it all started . . .

In the beginning there was God - and God created mankind. Mankind represents us all - boy/girl/young/old - so when you read this story you can put your name wherever it refers to mankind. God created mankind so that he could share his love with us and so that we could have a friendship with him. God was pleased with what he had made and thought that mankind was great. Equally, mankind thought God was pretty amazing too and they were best friends. This is how God intended it to be. Everything was perfect and God and mankind lived like this for some time - happy in paradise

- until one day mankind did something that changed everything.

Even though God had been nothing but caring and loving towards mankind, and had provided him with the perfect life and the best friend ever, mankind decided he wanted to go his own way and do his own thing. So mankind turned his back on God and paradise and went off and did things that God had warned him not to do. Mankind started to do bad things that he knew were wrong, and the result was that not only did he hurt himself and other people, but most of all, it ruined the perfect friendship he'd enjoyed with God.

It became impossible for mankind to have the same relationship with God again because the wrong things mankind had got involved in created a big barrier between him and God. The Bible calls these wrong things 'sin'. Sin is everything we've ever said, thought or done that is wrong and against God's ways and purposes for us. You may be thinking, 'Well I haven't been that bad, it's not like I've killed someone or something.' But the Bible says that *'All have sinned and are not good enough for God's glory'* (Romans 3:23). This basically means that all of us have done wrong whether something big or small, and God sees it all the same - as sin. Perhaps the biggest thing we have all done wrong is to have ignored God, turned our back on him and said that we don't want him involved in our lives, even though he was the one who made us! So all of us were in this position of being on the other side of the barrier - separated from God by our sin.

When God looked at the situation, he was gutted, because he knew that this bad stuff would lead mankind to an awful end. The Bible says, *'When people sin, they earn what sin pays - death'* (Romans 6:23). So, even though mankind had got himself into this mess, God decided to come up with a solution to stop mankind destroying himself and to get rid of the barrier of sin that kept them apart.

His solution was to send Jesus Christ to earth. Though Jesus is called the 'Son of God', he was also God himself in the flesh - God in human form. Jesus was sent to earth to show mankind a way out of their mess. No one seriously doubts that Jesus Christ existed - the Bible contains four books about his life and historical research has shown them to be reliable in what they tell us about Jesus. However, the question is, was he who he claimed to be - God in the flesh, God in human form?

Jesus did all sorts of amazing things in his time on earth (you can read about them in the books in the Bible about his life - Matthew, Mark, Luke and John) including healing people, speaking wise words and all sorts of miracles. However, Jesus said that his real purpose for being born was to die. Pretty strange thing to say, eh? What Jesus was referring to was the huge significance attached to his death.

You've probably heard the Easter story of when Jesus was executed by being nailed to a huge wooden cross (that's why we have hot cross buns at Easter by the way!). Well, a lot more was going on then than just a good man being executed for making some mad claims. Mankind deserved punishment for the wrong stuff they had done but, instead, Jesus took the blame for all the wrong stuff on himself, and took the punishment in mankind's place. Jesus was sentenced to death, even though he hadn't done anything wrong - ever - and was even found innocent at his trial. So when Jesus died, he paid the price once and for all, for all of mankind's sin and wrong-doing, thus removing the barrier between mankind and God. This meant that God could forgive mankind and that the way was now free again for mankind to have a friendship with God like before - if mankind wants it. God will not force anybody, it is up to each individual, but the opportunity is now there equally for everyone. It is a free gift that you can choose to accept or reject. *'God loved the world so much that he gave his one and only Son so that whoever believes in him may not be lost, but have eternal life'* (John 3:16).

Of course the story did not end there. Three days later Jesus was raised to life again - something we call the resurrection. Hundreds of people saw him alive again and were amazed, even though Jesus had told them that this would happen. The resurrection proved that Jesus really was who he said he was - no ordinary man would come back to life again. Shortly after this, Jesus told his followers that it was time for him to go back to be with his father in heaven. At first Jesus' mates were upset and didn't want him to go, but then he reassured them by telling them that it was actually better for them if he did go, and that he was going to leave behind a helper for them - the Holy Spirit. Jesus explained that if he stayed as he was, he could only be in one place at one time like any human. But if he were to go, he would leave behind the Holy Spirit to help and guide all Christians all over the world at the same time. It is the Holy Spirit (who is God within us) that we have with us today in the new millennium, and it is through the Holy Spirit that God guides us, speaks to us and shows himself in his power to us today.

A Christian is not a super human being who is perfect and has never done anything wrong. You do not have to be perfect to be a Christian.

A Christian is an ordinary person like you and me who has admitted that they've done wrong and who has asked Jesus into their lives to forgive them, for his friendship, and to help them to live 100 per cent for him. Not only do you get forgiven and get to be with him forever after you die, you also get a better life now with him helping you, guiding you and loving you every moment of every day. Jesus said, '*I came to give life - life in all its fullness*' (John 10:10). God has a specific plan and purpose just for you. So what are you waiting for?

Christians are not perfect, they're people who've been forgiven!

... and the prayer

Life to the full through a friendship with God is just one prayer away. You don't need any fancy or special words to pray, but you can use the words below and make them your own if it helps you:

God, I believe *that you are there and I'm sorry that I have spent so much of my life ignoring you.* **Thank you** *that you care about me and want to relate to me as a friend so much that* **you died for my sins**. *At the moment it feels like I hardly know you, but I really want to get to know you better.*

I know that in the time I've spent ignoring you I've screwed up a lot and done lots of things wrong. I wish they hadn't happened and I want you to know that I am sorry. **Please forgive me.**

Thank you Jesus that you died on the cross for me. I now give control of my life to you. I want to trust you completely with every part of my life and put you first. Holy Spirit, help me to **live my life 100 per cent for God** *and give me the strength to know him more as each day passes.*

Amen

If you prayed this prayer or one like it, God has totally forgiven you for everything you've done wrong and has accepted you as one of his own children. There is a party going on in heaven right now celebrating the fact that you have joined the family by becoming a Christian!

Now that you have prayed this prayer, it is a good idea to tell someone you know and trust in the next twenty-four hours.

What do I do now, and where do I go from here?

Though you've probably just made the most important decision of your life - and, might I add, the 'best' decision of your life - in many ways that was the easy bit. Now that you've made a commitment to God and decided to follow Jesus with your life, you may be feeling a little unsure of what you've decided. Let me reassure you that all of these feelings are perfectly normal. Being a Christian is all about having a friendship with God and I want to give you a few guidelines to help you know where to go from here and also what to expect. Living out your new life with Christ is not always an easy road but, believe me, it's worth it.

The best of best friends

Your new friendship with God is a bit like a marriage. It requires a commitment to the relationship from a motive of love, rather than just an agreement or contract. If you got married but then never spoke to your husband or wife, spent time with them, or tried to get to know them better, it wouldn't be much of a marriage would it? Instead, you would find out what they like, what pleases them and makes them happy and then you'd spend your time trying to do just that. It is the same with our new friendship with God. If we really want to make a go of it, then we want to find out more about God and how he wants us to live. Our aim in life, as a Christian, is to live a life that is pleasing to Him and to become more and more like Jesus. The Bible says, *'You are God's children whom he loves, so try to be like him'* (Ephesians 5:1) and *'In your lives you must think and act like Christ Jesus'* (Philippians 2:5). As I'm sure you can imagine, there are some distinct advantages to having the all-powerful God of the universe on your side as your best mate. Forget 'my dad's a policeman' - 'my dad's the creator of everything' is slightly cooler don't you think! But, joking aside, it is important that we realise that although God is absolutely huge and more amazing than we can even begin to get our head around, he is also interested in the tiniest details of our everyday lives - what concerns us, concerns him. He is 'King of kings' but also the *'friend that sticks closer than a brother'* (1Timothy 6:15). Basically, God is the best friend we can ever have. We can tell him absolutely anything and everything and he is always there for us and never lets us down. He is also a father to us - but not like our earthly fathers who sometimes make mistakes because they are human - God always knows what is best for us. He disciplines us like a father ' ... *God is treating you as children. All children are disciplined by their fathers'* (Hebrews 12:7-9) but he also loves us

'The night I became a **Christian** was the **best buzz** I have ever had.'

– Claire

'Changing my old bad ways and habits was one of the most difficult things when I first became a Christian, but I've got some really special Christian mates and they have helped me a lot. I realised that when I made a commitment to God it was about being a Christian 24/7 not just when I felt like it!'

— Abbey

and wants to look after us like a father *'How much more will your heavenly Father give good things to those who ask him'* (Matthew 7:9-11).

You may have heard Christians describing themselves as being 'born again'. This is because the Bible describes when we ask God into our lives as being re-born. 1 Peter 2:2 describes us as *'newborn babies'*. We start our lives again in a way - it is a new and fresh beginning when everything bad from our past can be left behind - but we have to learn how to live our new life with God. *'If anyone belongs to Christ, there begins a new creation. The old things have gone: everything is made new!'* (2 Corinthians 5:17). *'But you were taught to be made new in your hearts, to become a new person. That new person is made to be like God - made to be truly good and holy'* (Ephesians 4 :23-24).

A new life

This means we must be ready to make changes in our lives. But don't worry, this is not something you have to struggle with yourself or get right straight away. The most important thing is that you have made a commitment to God and have asked him into your life. God himself will help you to live it for him by his Holy Spirit and there is the help and support of Christian friends. You don't lose your personality when you become a Christian. You won't be expected to wear a cagoule or flowery dress, complete with white socks and sandals as soon as you make a commitment. You keep all the good things about your personality - that is how God made you. You are unique and God loves you as you are. The point is that God wants to help you get rid of all the not-so-good things about you and add a whole lot more good stuff in their place!

'I realised that you **shouldn't compare yourself** to anyone else and how they are doing. You have to **just listen to God** and to what he wants for you, personally, which means learning to understand when God is trying to tell you something.'

— David

'I realise now that I **can still have just as much fun, or even more, being a Christian.** I can still keep all my mates and have as much fun, but now I just have some guidance and back-up to help me.'

— Abbey

Ephesians 4:21-24 gives us a helpful formula to adapt to a new way of living that is pleasing to God: *'I know that you heard about him, and you are in him, so you were taught the truth that is in Jesus. You were taught to leave your old self - to stop living the evil way you lived before. That old self becomes worse, because people are fooled by the evil things they want to do. But you were taught to be made new in your hearts, to become a new person. That new person is made to be like God - made to be truly good and holy.'*

Just trying to do what we think is the right thing won't work - we must make the decision to leave our old way of living first. It would be like trying to fit a brand new set of clothes over lots of layers of old shabby ones - it would be uncomfortable and would restrict your movement. However, if we let Jesus take away the old clothes - all the wrong we've done or are doing - he will then give us just one garment to wear that is new and wonderful and comfortable. (Often in the Bible, Jesus' righteousness is described as gleaming-white linen garments that he gives us to wear: this was considered one of the finest materials of the time.) Once we have done that, we can then change and be made new in the attitude of our minds and in our hearts, and then start to add the new, good things into our lives.

First of all, there is something to leave behind and put off - our old self, then something to change - our

Remember the formula -

....

● something to leave/put off - old self

● something to change - attitude of mind and heart

● something to become/put on - new self

attitude of mind and heart, and then something to become, put on - our new self.

Another way of thinking of it is like a car being converted from running on the old leaded petrol to running on the new unleaded fuel. It would not work to simply start adding unleaded petrol whilst still using leaded. You would need to first stop using the old leaded petrol that is bad for the environment (our wrong and old ways of living), then convert the car ready to receive different fuel (our change of heart to follow Jesus) and finally add the new, cleaner unleaded petrol (the things of God - his ways and living for him).

However, it is important to know that God does not wait for us to be perfect before he loves and accepts us. Romans 5:8 tells us that '*Jesus died for us while we were still sinners*'

- that means while we were still doing wrong. Some things you may have been doing, or ways you may have been living may take a while to change, and that is OK. The main thing is that you have asked Jesus into your life and, as long as you are open to him and want him to, he will gradually help you to change at a pace that he knows is right for you. He will highlight things in you to change as and when he knows you are ready to do so. It is important that you understand this and are not forced by others to change at a faster pace than you can cope with. At the same time, you must not avoid things in you that you know need changing. Get someone (an older Christian friend or youth leader) to help you to work through these issues on an on-going, regular basis.

'One of the things that held me back from becoming a Christian at first was that I wanted to do a good job at being a Christian and I didn't think I could do it. But somebody told me that **God does not want to wait until you are perfect, you can just come as you are.** That really helped me and started to boost my confidence.'

— Abbey

'Some of my friends at school took the mickey out of me when I became a Christian and that was quite hard, but all my closest friends were **really cool** about it and were happy for me.'

— Claire

You are not alone

If we try to change solely in our own strength we will not be able to keep it up, but the good news is that we are not alone. As well as help from others, we have a much greater helper; an invisible and powerful friend - the Holy Spirit. After Jesus was raised to life and before he returned to heaven to be with his father, he promised that he would not leave us alone: *'I will ask the Father, and he will give you another Helper to be with you for ever - the Spirit of truth . . . he lives with you and he will be in you'* (John 14:16-17). The Holy Spirit is not like a floaty 'Casper the friendly ghost'. He is God coming to live in us to help us and to guide us as soon as we ask Jesus into our lives. We can't see him, but we know he is there because we feel him guiding us. The Holy Spirit is a bit like your new conscience that helps you to know what is right, what is wrong, and what pleases God. We can ask the Holy Spirit to help us to act in the right way in situations, to help us make important decisions, and to generally help us to live our lives in the right way for God. *'But you are not ruled by your sinful selves. You are ruled by the Spirit, if that Spirit of God really lives in you'* (Romans 8:9). *'Live by following the Spirit. Then you will not do what your sinful selves want'* (Galatians 5:16). When the Holy Spirit is active in our lives, we start to live our life in a way that is pleasing to God: *'But the Spirit produces the fruit of love, joy, peace, patience, kindness, goodness, faithfulness, gentleness, self-control'* (Galatians 5:22-23). The Holy Spirit can make a really big difference in our lives. Through him, God is always with us, so that we are never alone. Our part is to keep in touch with him and listen to him: making sure that we do not ignore his presence in our lives. *'We get our new life from the Spirit, so we should follow the Spirit'* (Galatians 5:25).

Often when people say that God has spoken to them it is the Holy Spirit giving them a deep 'knowing' of something that they didn't know.

WORDS FROM THE SHINE GIRLS:

'I remember that the day after I became a Christian I was having doubts and thinking, "how do I know if this is true?" But I also remember thinking, "if it is true then I definitely don't want to miss out on this - it sounds amazing!" I felt that I would only know if I tried it, so I decided to stick at it and God has been with me and proved himself real to me time and time again.'

— Loretta

Talking to God - prayer

'It's good to talk!' was the famous slogan for a British Telecom campaign which had more than just a few pearls of wisdom in it. Most of us agree that communication is a good thing - after all, we don't get very far without it. You don't get that top you wanted for your birthday, to go out with the boy/girl you fancy or that shoulder to cry on, without communication. Any kind of relationship needs communication if it is to be a successful one. Your best mate wouldn't be too happy if you never talked to them about what's going on in your life, and sometimes we need to ask for help, to simply share what's on our mind, or share some exciting news. If you are a Christian (or thinking about becoming one), it is basically all about having a friendship with God. This means you need to start talking to him. This is called *prayer*.

There are many myths about prayer such as, you have to kneel down by the side of your bed with your eyes closed and hands together and use big, long, fancy words - NOT SO! *Prayer is simply chatting to God.*

Prayer is simply chatting to God.

This means you talk to him just like you'd talk to your best mate, except it's better because you can talk to him anytime and anywhere about absolutely anything and everything.

Did you know that Prayer ...

- doesn't have to be out loud, it can be in your head?
- doesn't have to be on your own, you can pray together with a group of friends?
- doesn't have to be a shopping list (a list of things you ask God for all the time)?
- can tell God about things going on in your life or let him know how great he is?
- can be to thank God for things that have gone well or where he has helped you?

God always hears your prayers, always listens and always answers them. However, it may not always be in the way you want him to answer them or expect. Someone once said that God answers prayers in one of three ways, which can be easily remembered as being like traffic light signals:

RED
STOP = 'NO'
(That's not my will for
you or good for you)

AMBER
WAIT = 'YES, BUT NOT YET'
(In God's
perfect timing)

GREEN
GO = 'YES!'

So be prepared to accept whatever God's answer might be. But remember, he always knows what's best and always wants what's best for you.

I can remember a series of significant answers to prayer when I particularly needed to hear from God over my future just after I'd finished my A levels. I had applied to university to do media studies and journalism, when what I really wanted was a career in singing. But this seemed unrealistic to me and my teachers even advised me so. I had to agree with them that it seemed more like a dream than a conceivable ambition. However, I couldn't get away from the fact that singing was my heart's desire. Surely, that was an indication of my life-calling, wasn't it?

I got offers from all of the universities I applied to, but then I received a letter to say one of my chosen courses was not running any more. In the meantime, I had found a more practical course and had thought to myself, this is my chance not to be

So I said to God: 'OK ...'

stuck doing something I don't really want to do for three years. So I said to God: 'OK, I don't mind going to university, if I can do this new, more practical course I have found'.

I applied, feeling quite confident that I would be accepted, as the required grades were low in comparison to the other courses that had already offered me places. So, you can imagine how devastated I was when the slip was returned with a big 'REJECTED' stamp on it. I couldn't understand it. Why had God allowed me to be accepted for the courses I didn't want to do, which needed high grades, but rejected from the only one I really wanted that required much lower grades? I was disappointed and confused so I decided to pray.

At first, I felt nothing, and then a song came into my head. I gradually realised that God was trying to tell me something through a deep 'knowing' and peace that I most definitely did not have before. He seemed to be saying, 'Trust in me, because I love you'. I couldn't explain it, but I just knew it was God talking to me. I felt totally different about the whole thing.

Now, at first, nothing changed, but two weeks later it did. There were only a few weeks left before I was due to go to university. While I was reading a magazine, an advert leaped out at me, cartoon-style. It said, 'Are you a Christian and want to learn to Sing and dance? Auditions being held for the School of Creative Ministries - Christian Performing Arts school.' I knew this was for me! I then went for my first ever audition - and passed!

The next hurdle was the fees - a couple of hundred pounds that I didn't have. So again, I prayed about it. Over the next couple of weeks, I miraculously got the money for the first term through anonymous gifts and donations from friends and family. I decided that I would trust God for the other two terms. So off I went to London and had an amazing year growing closer to God and receiving training for the Arts. As a result of this year, I got my first ever session work as part of a choir singing with Sting and M People at the Brit Awards and then I went on to join the World Wide Message Tribe which led on to being a part of Shine. By praying, God heard me, guided me and opened doors for me to reach my heart's desire.

When you pray, you can either pray to God as your Father or to Jesus as your friend - Jesus said we could ask the Father for things in his (Jesus') name. You can also pray to the Holy Spirit, particularly if you need God's power for a situation, to guide you or be with you to help you.

In case you are a little lost for words at times and are not sure quite what to say to God or where to start, here are a few prayers that you can use, on a few different subjects that you might face. But remember - you do not have to use any special formula to pray - you can talk to God in your own words any time, and that is more than good enough! Oh, and in case you were wondering ...

If you find praying difficult . . .

- Try having a prayer timetable of different things you want to cover in prayer, e.g.

MON....	*Family*
TUES....	*Friends*
WEDS...	*Thank God*
THURS..	*People who need help*
FRI......	*Help to live for God*
SAT......	*World Issues*
SUN.....	*Church Life*

- Try fixing a specific time to pray each day (e.g. before you go to bed or before school/work)
- Try starting a 'prayer triplet' - meeting regularly with two other friends, to pray together
- Try going out for a walk somewhere quiet and praying
- Try putting on some Christian or worship music as you pray
- Try praying short prayers throughout the day rather than a set long period

'Amen' means 'so let it be'.

● Temptation

Lord, you know everything about me, including my weaknesses. Please give me the strength to overcome all things that pull me away from you, especially _____ that I am struggling with at the moment. Help me to keep away from situations that make it difficult for me to stay strong. Thank you that you always love me. Please be with me today and guide me in my thoughts, words and actions.

Amen

'The only temptation that has come to you is that which everyone has. But you can trust God, who will not let you be tempted more than you can stand. But when you are tempted, he will also give you a way to escape so that you will be able to stand it.'

(1 Corinthians 10:13)

● Doubts

Lord, lately I have been having some doubts. I've experienced you in my life so I know you are there. Please help me to feel you are there. Let me feel you with me every moment of the day. Help me to speak to someone who can help me to find answers to my questions, so that I won't have reason to doubt anymore. Thank you because I know you died on the Cross and that you love me enough to do this for me.

Amen

'Then Jesus told him [Thomas, his disciple], 'You believe because you see me. Those who believe without seeing me will be truly happy'.

(John 20:29)

● Family

Thank you Lord for my family. Even though we have our ups and downs, I thank you that you have put people around me who care for me. Sometimes though, I find it really difficult, because it feels as if my family doesn't understand me or the things I'm going through. Please help me not to take out my frustration on them or have a bad attitude towards them, but please also help them to meet me half way. Thank you that I have you as my heavenly father and that you are always there for me. Thank you that you love me as a perfect father would. Help me to be a good child for you and for them.

Amen

....

'Children obey your parents as the Lord wants, because this is the right thing to do. The command says, "Honour your father and mother". This is the first command that has a promise with it - "Then everything will be well with you, and you will have a long life on the earth". '
(Ephesians 6:1-3)

● Friendship/ Relationships

Lord, thank you for my friends and all the people you have placed in my life who are important to me. Help me to treat people as you would want me to, help me to forgive others as you have forgiven me and to put their needs before my own. Help me to be kind to everyone, but give me wisdom to befriend those that will draw me closer to you and to spend less time with those that make it difficult for me to follow you.

Amen.

....

'A friend loves you all the time, and a brother helps in time of trouble.'
(Proverbs 17:17)

'Some friends may ruin you, but a real friend will be more loyal than a brother.'
(Proverbs 18:24)

● Putting God first

God, sometimes it is so easy to become swamped by life, and sometimes I allow myself to get too busy and forget to give you the time you deserve. I know that you always have time for me, though, and I want to make you first priority in my life. If there is anything in my life that I hold as more important than you or that distracts me from you, please show it to me and show me how to deal with it. Lord, help me to have you at the centre of my life and to build everything else around you. Thank you for your promise that if I put you first, then you will take care of everything else.

Amen

....

'The thing you should want most is God's Kingdom and doing what God wants. Then all these other things you need will be given to you.'

(Matthew 6:33)

● Struggling with living out being a Christian

Thank you Jesus that you died for me and that you loved me enough to do that. Help me to live my life for you 100 per cent. Sometimes I find it so hard to be what you would want me to be every day, but please help me to try my best and to aim to be more like you. Help me not to go back to doing things that I used to do before I knew you. Thank you that life to the full is only found in you - and I don't want to miss out on that. Fill me with your Holy Spirit every day to enable me to be what you would want me to be.

Amen

....

'Do not change yourselves to be like the people of this world, but be changed within by a new way of thinking. Then you will be able to decide what God wants for you; you will know what is good and pleasing to him and what is perfect.'

(Romans 12:2)

● Sharing faith/ telling others

Lord, you have made such a difference in my life that I don't want to just keep you to myself. Help me to have boldness and not to miss an opportunity to talk about you with friends and family who don't yet know you personally. Please let the subject come up in a natural way and give me the right words to say and the answers for any questions they may have. Most of all Lord, may you SHOW in my life by shining through me in everything I do.

Amen

'You are a light that gives light to the world. . . . you should be a light for other people. Live so that they will see the good things you do and will praise your Father in heaven.'

(Matthew 5:14-16)

● Forgiveness

Lord, lately I have strayed from your path and have gone wrong, doing things and acting in ways that I know I shouldn't. I'm sorry! Thank you, though, that you died for me on the cross and forgive me for all my wrongs. Help me to live a life worthy of who you have now made me - a new creation! Help me not to keep making the same mistakes, and help me to accept that you have forgiven me and to move on. Thank you for your grace - the undeserved favour of God.

Amen

'Create in me a pure heart, God, and make my spirit right again. Do not send me away from you or take your Holy Spirit away from me. Give me back the joy of your salvation. Keep me strong by giving me a willing spirit.'

(Psalm 51:10-12)

● Future

Thank you Lord that my life is in your hands. You know my dreams and heart's desires and that I really want to please you with what I do with my life. Please guide my thoughts and help me to make wise choices concerning the future. It seems so scary right now, but I know you have everything in control. Help me not to worry about it, but to trust in you.

Amen

....

'Depend on the Lord in whatever you do, and your plans will succeed.'
(Proverbs 16:3)

So you can see that you don't have to use fancy long words to pray, just chat to God in your own words. Jesus has some great advice for us on the subject of prayer: *'When you pray, you should go into your room and close the door and pray to your Father who cannot be seen. Your Father can see what is done in secret, and he will reward you. And when you pray, don't be like those people who don't know God. They continue saying things that mean nothing, thinking that God will hear them because of their many words. Don't be like them, because your Father knows the things you need before you ask him'* (Matthew 6:6-8).

WORDS FROM THE SHINE GIRLS:

'I know, without a doubt, that when you pray, things happen. If I could only tell you how much it's changed my life! God hears every prayer and he won't ever let you down - although he might not answer in the way you expect.'

— Hanne

A map book for life

Starting to read the Bible can seem very daunting at first, and perhaps a little boring, because it is so big. However, there are lots of things that can help you.

The Bible is God's word to us and is therefore very important. It is a bit like a map book for life - our own manual and guide to living this life the best way - as God wants us to. It has information, instructions and answers on most things that you come across in life. It really is quite an amazing book - but it is so much more than just a book. Although God himself did not physically write the Bible, he did inspire all of the writers

31

to pen its contents. The Bible says that *'All Scripture is given by God and is useful for teaching, for showing people what is wrong in their lives, for correcting faults and for teaching how to live right. Using the Scriptures, the person who serves God will be capable, having all that is needed to do every good work'* (2 Timothy 3:16-17). The Bible is made up of 66 different short books from history books, to poetry books, to books telling about the future. It is split into two main sections - the Old Testament (before Jesus was born) and the New Testament (after Jesus was born).

The Bible is described as 'God's living word' because it is more than just writing on pages, it is powerful and life-giving: *'God's word is alive and working and is sharper than a double-edged sword. It cuts all the way into us, where the soul and the spirit are joined, to the centre of our joints and bones. And it judges the thoughts and feelings in our hearts'* (Hebrews 4:12).

The Gospels are a good place to start as they tell us about, Jesus' life

The Gospels - Matthew, Mark, Luke and John - are a good place to start, as they tell you all about the life of Jesus. You can find them in the New Testament (the second half of the Bible). There are special youth versions of the Bible and also youth study notes, all written in today's language, so it is easier to understand and designed to help you get the most out of reading the Bible. I recommend the Youth Bible - New Century Version published by Word. All Bible quotes in this book are from the Youth Bible. Most Christian bookshops will have them, as will many general bookshops. If they don't have it they can order you one in.

The more we read the Bible, the more we begin to understand God's design for life and how to live it to the full. It helps us to keep on the right track: *'How can a young person live a pure life? By obeying your word'* (Psalm 119:9). The Bible is also the main way that God can 'speak' to us, by communicating his views and advice on all the things we face, as well as giving us warnings and guidance. It also tells us how much God loves us and what he thinks of us.

The first time I ever felt God **speaking directly to me,** was through the **Bible.**

God can speak to us through the Bible

The first time I ever felt God speaking directly to me, was through the Bible. I had not been a Christian for very long - a matter of months - when I attended a youth event where some young Christians from America were over in the UK singing and dancing and performing drama sketches in schools and talking about their faith. The group made such an impact on me that I remember praying 'God this is so what I want to do with my life. If I can use my love for singing and dancing and tell others about you at the same time, that would be my dream come true.' I went home that night and prayed to God that one day he would give me my heart's desire. I then opened my Bible desperate to hear from God. To my amazement, the page it opened on directly spoke to me. It was Ecclesiastes 11:9, and was titled 'Advice to Young People'. It said, *'Young people, enjoy yourselves while*

33

you are young; be happy while you are young. Do whatever your heart desires, whatever you want to do. But remember that God will judge you for everything you do.' I was amazed. I couldn't believe how God was so concerned with me and my dreams, enough to tell me, all but outright, to go for it! I held on to that promise from God and, as you know, he gave me my heart's desire and now I am working in Shine where I get to use all the things I love: music, singing and dancing, along with the other most important thing in my life - my friendship with God.

That was just one example of when God has spoken to me through the Bible, but there have been many other times when he has used the Bible to guide, warn or answer me about other things.

Here are some answers to a few of the commonly asked questions concerning the Bible:

* What if I don't understand it?

Before you read the Bible, ask God to help you to understand what you are about to read and how to get the most out of it. Try re-writing what you have read, but write what you think it is saying in your own words. If you are really stuck, ask a Christian friend or youth leader to explain it to you.

* How often should I read it?

There is no set time or amount that you should read the Bible, but the more regularly you read it, the more what you are reading starts to stick in your mind - and the more that happens, the more you have answers to other people's questions and know what to do, yourself, in different situations. Furthermore, the more we read the Bible, the more we get to know God and how to live our lives for him, and the more our faith will grow. So, there are many advantages to getting into a routine of reading the Bible regularly. However, don't set yourself so much to read that you get bored or don't take it in because it's too much to remember. But, at the same time, always try to read in sections rather than individual verses that can be taken out of context. This way, you get the whole picture of what is being said, including the background and setting.

the more we **read the Bible** the more we get to **know God**

* When should I read the Bible?

As with finding a suitable prayer time, each case will be individual to each lifestyle. However, a good tip is: don't read the Bible when you are really tired - you won't be able to concen- trate or remember what you've read. So, if you know you are not a morning person and don't usually wake up until break-time, perhaps breakfast reading is not the slot for you. Equally, if you love your bed, perhaps last thing at night is not your ideal time. Find a suitable time and place where you won't be disturbed.

* What should I read in the Bible?

The Bible is not like a novel that you would read from front to back, cover to cover. It is made up of lots of separate and very different books and each one stands on its own, so you can pick any book to start working through. As I mentioned before, the Gospels Matthew, Mark, Luke and John, in the New Testament (the second half of the Bible), are a good place to start, as they tell us all about Jesus' life. We can get to know him better by reading about the things he did and what he was like. If we want to know what God lots of **separate** and very different **books** and each one stands on its own

is like, we can look at Jesus; the Bible says *'No one can see God, but Jesus Christ is exactly like him. He ranks higher than anything that has been made'* (Colossians 1:15). Jesus also said *'Whoever has seen me has seen the Father'* (John 14:9).

Some of the books near the beginning of the Bible, in the Old Testament, can be a little heavy going for new Christians. So it might be a good idea to leave them until you have been a Christian for a little while. Having said that, Genesis (the first book of the Bible) is a great book to read to see how it all started! So pick one book to start working through and, perhaps, set yourself the goal of reading a chapter a day. If you cope with that OK, why not read one of the Psalms each day as well. Psalms are songs and poems written by all sorts of people and cover many subjects from praise, to encouragement, to help. They can be very uplifting and are fairly easy reading. You can find the book of Psalms in the

Old Testament, towards the middle of the Bible. Try getting into the habit of memorising bits of the Bible. Start with a short verse or two. Once it is in your memory, it can have more effect in your life.

Remember, don't worry if you miss a day, God is not holding a score chart on you!

✱ How do I apply the Bible to my life daily?

Even though the Bible was written hundreds of years ago, it is called 'God's living word' because it is still relevant to our lives today. God's word will never fade out or go out of date. Admittedly, there are cultural differences, where times have moved on, but the basic principles of living still stand just as strong today. The Bible is full of help, advice, and answers on things like relationships, sex, money, careers and most other issues that we face today. In all situations, it is important that we know what God thinks on the subject, what he wants us to do, and how he wants us to be. All this is in the Bible. One exercise which may help you apply God's word to your life, is to write out what you have read in the Bible and try applying it to a situation you are in or may face in your life. Write down what you think the verses are saying to you and how that would help you, or what it shows you about something you are dealing with in your life. Look at the life of Jesus or of other characters in the Bible, and see how they reacted in situations, or how God helped them.

Never be afraid to ask an older Christian friend or youth leader for help if you are struggling with the Bible.

WORDS FROM THE SHINE GIRLS:

'The Bible is full of good advice and guidance for life. It sometimes has the bad image of being just a book full of a load of rules and regulations that are there to spoil our fun. However, most of the lessons we can learn from people's experiences in the Bible and the teachings of Jesus are there to protect us and show us how to live life in a way that is not only best for us, but is also pleasing to God.

— Tash

Many people have a typical picture (stereotype) of what they think church is like and what it is all about. Sometimes those stereotypes can have some truth in them, but often they are just a distorted picture of what it's really about. My earliest memory of church was being dragged along to Sunday school when I was about 5 years old and being bored out of my brain. As you can imagine, I was not too keen to go again.

My next encounter with church was not until I was 14. My mum had just become a Christian and asked my sister and me to go to church with her. She was keen that we didn't just go on what our friends at school had said - or even what she had told us about it - she wanted us to form our own opinion of church and Christianity for ourselves, from our own experience. We agreed that this was fair enough. Well, I agreed to go along, expecting it to be very boring, with creepy church organ music and filled with old ladies in their hats and gloves looking down their glasses at me. I couldn't have been more wrong! Yes, it was strange, but boring it most certainly was not. The church I went to was filled with people of all ages, including other teenagers, and the music was provided by a live band, complete with drums and electric guitar! I was not used to seeing people dancing around and singing to Jesus, but I could see that these people definitely had something that I didn't. My stereotype of church had been very wrong.

What is Church for?

I'd like to dispel a few more myths. Going to church is not what makes you a Christian - you could go to church every Sunday of your life and it would not make you a Christian. Believing in Jesus and what he's done for you by dying for you is what makes you a Christian. Christians go to church because it is good for them

It's important to find a Church that is right and suitable for YOU!

Church is not a building, it's a group of Christians

and because they want to, not because they have to. For example, if you are a Manchester United fan, it is not a chore to go to Old Trafford to see them play - you want to go, no one has to force you. In the same way, church is a great place to learn more about God, grow closer to him and to spend time with other Christians.

Church is not a building, as many may think, church is a gathering of Christians. So you can have 'church' by meeting together with other Christian friends during the week, not just on Sundays.

There are many different types of Christian churches, because there are many different types of Christian people. Some people like to worship God in a quiet meditative way, while others like to worship in a loud all-singing all-dancing manner. No

church is better or more right in God's eyes. The question is, which church is right and suitable for YOU.

Church can be a bit of a culture shock at first, so try to go with people you know. If it's a church that loves Jesus and teaches the Bible, has people of your age, and if you stick it out, you will definitely get lots out of it. You may be surprised and find that you enjoy it!

'Now I am a Christian, I don't think that Church is boring any more. I used to think it was just full of old people, with a choir. It is more fun than I thought it would be.'

— Claire

Youth Groups

It is very important that you begin to spend time with other Christians that you can talk to and who can help you. It's also fun meeting other Christians your own age, as you can help each other. The person who gave you this book should be able to put you in touch with a good church youth group in your area. There will be people who would love to get to know you and help you in your new friendship with God, or anything else you may need. One of the things that were most helpful to me when I first became a Christian was the church youth group. I attended it from age 14 until I was 18 years old. Not only did we have a good laugh and lots of fun, but I also made some lifelong friends and got a great foundation of knowledge about Jesus and the Bible at a pace I could handle.

'Because none of my old friends are Christians, I know it would really help me to make Christian friends with people I feel I can be myself with as a new Christian.'

– Claire

It is also a good idea to attend a 'new Christians' group or course, if there is one running. This way you don't feel that you are the only one just starting out, and can be with other people who are asking the same questions. It is also encouraging to learn with others, and progress and grow together.

'My Christian friends have really helped me. **They are totally normal people,** and most of them have been through the same problems as me, so that's useful. **I trust them** and I can ask them stuff and know that their advice is sound! Even if I feel like I'm asking them a stupid question, I **don't feel embarrassed**. Some of them are my role models.'

– Abbey

'My youth group was what helped me the most when I first became a Christian. The **youth leader** spent a lot of time teaching us from the Bible and **helping us to understand** some very complex issues. He answered all the questions I had. My youth group was a place that I felt that I could make mistakes and learn in a **safe** environment. I know that without the **help and support** that I constantly received, and am still receiving, from my leaders and friends, I would not be here now as a Christian. Church, and especially the youth group, helped me so much to have a **greater understanding of Jesus** and who he is.'

42   – Lucy

Someone to look up to

No matter how determined you are to make it, there are going to be times when you're finding it tough to be a Christian and will need some extra help. That's why it is a good idea to begin to develop a friendship with someone who you can be accountable to. This person should be someone you know and trust, who has been a Christian for longer than you have. If they are older than you are, it also makes it easier for them to help you. A youth leader is a great choice for this role, for all of the above reasons, but it doesn't have to be. Make sure you are regularly in touch with this person: ask them any questions you have, and talk to them about any problems that may come up. Talking is a great help, but having someone like this praying with you and for you is even better. Don't be worried about asking someone if they can fulfil this role (disciple you) - any older Christian will feel very privileged to be asked, and will enjoy helping you to get the most out of your new life with God.

'Having an older Christian to talk to and ask my questions to has helped me. I needed to have what Jesus had done on the Cross explained to me, and needed to be able to ask my questions privately without feeling like they were stupid. In the beginning, I didn't know how to pray and felt like I needed to be perfect straight away. By talking and asking questions I have begun to understand what it's really all about and what is important.'

— Claire

'I think an essential piece of equipment in your Christian life is someone to disciple you (like a mentor). It is what helped me the most to stick at being a Christian. Having someone to talk to who is more experienced in their Christian life than me, who can see my heart and knows me better than most people, was a massive help. They are someone I can trust and be totally, 100 per cent honest with, and who is not afraid to pull me up sometimes, and answer the millions of questions that I throw at them. That person — for me — is my youth leader. When there was stuff I didn't understand, or stuff I needed to deal with, and when things got tough at home, she helped me through it and kept me on the right track. When I felt that God was sooooooo far away and I didn't want to be a Christian anymore, she was there to guide and support me — even though I didn't want her to at the time!'

— Lucy

WORDS FROM THE SHINE GIRLS:

'When I first made a commitment to God, and started my new life as a Christian, youth group was my lifeline! Not only did I have a whole bunch of new friends, but I also had a safe, helpful environment in which to take my first steps as a Christian. There were people there to support me, involve me, and who I could follow and look up to until I felt more able to stand by myself.'

— Tash

Telling others—
sharing your faith

Once you begin to settle into your new life with God, you should start to share it with other people that don't know him. Like any good news, you will want to share him with the world. For example, if you had the cure to cancer it would not be fair - neither would you want - to keep it to yourself. Likewise, the brilliant news about Jesus and what he has done is for everybody and, in a way, we have a responsibility to share that with as many people as we come into contact with. Telling others about Jesus is called *evangelism*. So why is this so important, and why should we tell others about Jesus?

Why should we tell others about Jesus?

Jesus commanded us to do so. In Matthew 28:19 Jesus tells his disciples (his followers - so that means you too) to *'go and make followers of all people in the world. Baptise them in the name of the Father and the Son and the Holy Spirit.'* So we should 'evangelise' out of obedience to Jesus, because he tells us to. But we should also do so out of a desire to see others experiencing the great life that we enjoy with Jesus at the centre. The other reason is to ensure that others have the chance to accept Christ, be saved from hell and receive eternal life through him.

Evangelising may seem a bit of a scary prospect to you at the moment, but you needn't worry. For starters, it is not something that you have to do in a forced and unnatural way. If Jesus is central and, in fact, the most important thing in your life, then he will shine through you anyway. When Jesus is in your life he will affect all areas of it and others will see that in your speech, behaviour and in your way of handling situations. There are many ways that are far more effective than standing on the dining tables at lunch time and preaching to your whole school, so breathe a sigh of relief. Often, the best way to share Jesus with your friends is to show them rather than to tell them. This means letting them see Jesus in your life by the way you act in different situations and the things you join in or don't join in on. This gives a clearer message than merely forcing your opinions on others in a judgmental way. All that would do is earn you the nickname 'Bible-basher'. It is important not to behave towards your friends as though you think you are better than they are.

There are many ways to tell others about Jesus and there will certainly

Like any **good** news, you will want to **share Jesus** with the world be one that suits you and will come so naturally to you that you won't even realise you are doing it! As for *how* to do this - there is no set way, but here is some basic advice which might help you:

How should we tell others about Jesus?

Perhaps the best advice concerning telling others about your faith is to *be yourself*! Don't act in a way or use words you wouldn't normally, either to try to impress, or to fit in with the people you are talking to. Just share what Jesus has done in your life in a natural way. The biggest tool for evangelism you have is your life story (your testimony). How and why you came to know Jesus is totally personal to you and no one can argue with that, add to, or take away from it. Tell them a little bit about what you were like before you became a Christian, how and why you came to know Jesus, and then something of what your life has been like since. Make sure you don't waffle on though, practise it, and aim to keep it down to around three minutes.

Another tip is not to try to work or force Jesus into every conversation you have with people, in an unnatural way. Don't make people projects to convert, but seek to be a friend first and foremost, this way you will be

your **life story** is your **most powerful tool for** telling others about **Jesus**

'Some of my friends at school took the mickey out of me when I **became a Christian** and that was quite hard, but all my closest friends were really cool about it and were happy for me.'

– Claire

more effective and people are more likely to listen when the subject does come up. Again, if Jesus is central to your life, the subject will come up naturally sooner or later especially when those around you see the amazing change and good things that God is doing in your life. At the same time, don't be ashamed of your faith or try to hide the fact that you are a Christian. Jesus was not embarrassed about you when he died on the cross for you. So make sure that you are bold about sharing him with other people - you never know you may be a part of changing their life forever!

Be honest - be prepared to tell people what the 'difference' is in your life when they ask. Don't miss an opportunity through panic or embarrassment to share about what Jesus has done in your life. Equally, if you do not know the answer to a question someone asks you, just be honest and say so. You can then offer to find out for them, from an older Christian or youth leader who may know.

Be bold, but not arrogant. You may be worried about being picked on or taken the mickey out of for saying you're a Christian. But remember, a bully will bully about anything. When others see that you are not embarrassed about it, they will begin to respect you for your beliefs. If they don't, then they are too immature and should be ignored. Before I was a Christian, I was known for having a big mouth and being vocal about my opinions, so when I became a Christian I was pretty much the same, except I talked about Jesus instead and was always ready to answer any questions that any one would ask me.

'I thought that my friends would make fun of me, but actually, as we have got older, I've found they don't mind and are **curious** about why I go to Church. Most of them are **cool** about my beliefs, which was quite surprising to me.'

– Abbey

Let's take a look at some advice from the Bible on evangelism:

'Pray that I can speak in a way that will make it clear, as I should. Be wise in the way you act with people who are not believers, making the most of every opportunity. When you talk, you should always be kind and pleasant so you will be able to answer everyone in the way you should' (Colossians 4:4-6).

People's stereotypes of church and Christianity can put people off. This is because, unfortunately, somewhere along the line there has sometimes been some truth in those stereotypes. However, a true and clear picture of Jesus Christ generally does the opposite. You only have to take a look in the Bible to see how amazing Jesus was and is, and how people were drawn to him. So, our job is to make sure we are good imitators of him and show a good picture. Let's represent him well!

WORDS FROM THE SHINE GIRLS:

'**Telling others about Jesus** can either be the **cringiest** or the **easiest** thing that you can ever do. If your faith is truly part of you then nothing needs to be forced. **Be confident!** You've found something **amazing**, and the less embarrassed you are, the more other people will wonder **what it is that you've got!**'

– Nic

Questions, doubts and fears

7

This chapter aims to cover the most common questions, doubts and fears that I have come across in my work with Shine.

The whole point of this book is to help you to get the best start you possibly can in your new life with God. That means you must feel free to have doubts and feel able to ask questions too. It is not wrong to have questions. In fact they can help you to grow in your faith, as you learn more when you find out the answers.

● **Do I have to follow loads of rules and are there things I can't do as a Christian?**

Christianity isn't just a list of dos and don'ts, although there are guidelines that are there to help us, because God knows what is best for us. There is a Bible verse that says: *"'We are allowed to do all things," but all things are not good for us to do. "We are allowed to do all things," but not all things help others grow stronger. Do not look out only for yourselves. Look out for the good of others also'* (1 Corinthians 10:23-24). This means that God gives us the freedom we want, but he wants us to use that freedom wisely. Also, it is worth noting that the so-called 'rules' are often misquoted, and so people miss the point as they take them out of context. For example, many people think that the Bible says 'do not drink alcohol', when what it actually says is, *'do not get drunk'* (Ephesians 5:18). God has nothing against drinking (if you're of legal age), but what he does advise is common sense. We all know why it is not a good idea to get drunk: we do stupid things, make fools of ourselves and can even end up hurting ourselves and others - sometimes fatally! At first, it can be difficult to understand why God says that things like getting drunk and having sex outside of marriage are not a good idea, especially if this has been 'normal' for us before we experienced God. However, with a bit of thought we can work out why God advises us on most things - it's because he knows what's best for us and wants us to experience that to the full.

'A friend explained to me that in the Bible Jesus' disciples were **actually looking at him** after he was raised from the dead but they still doubted. When I heard that, it helped me to accept that it was **OK to have doubts** and that there were going to be **some questions** that I just wouldn't have the answers to.'

– David

51

● What if I can't give up my old ways straight away?

It would be too much for us and God doesn't expect us to completely change everything at once, especially if we want lasting results. As soon as you ask Jesus into your life, you receive the Holy Spirit (see chapter 2). *'Whoever confesses that Jesus is the Son of God has God living inside, and that person lives in God'* (1 John 4:15). The Holy Spirit himself will change you in many ways - and possibly quite quickly - within your first year of you being a Christian.

When we receive Jesus we begin to understand what is good for us and what isn't, and we want to work at adapting our lives to please him. So if we have been doing specific things that we know are not good, such as smoking, stealing and fighting, it is usually not too difficult to deal with these things fairly early on in our life as a Christian.

However, it is more difficult to change things like our attitudes and ways of thinking, because human beings are creatures of habit. You see, God changes our hearts, but we have to work on changing our minds to catch up with that. A good place to start is realising that being a Christian means giving God complete control over your life. He is not just an extra on top of the rest of your life; he should be the centre of everything. It takes a while to maintain a consistent and steady relationship with Jesus, and sometimes you may feel like it's just not happening at all. It is common to have an initial period when you seem to sail through, followed by times of being up and down and having many doubts and questions - this is normal!

The main thing is to realise that it is not your performance (your behaviour) that determines whether you are

> God **changes our hearts,** but we have to work on **changing our minds** to catch with that

a Christian or not, it is your heart. God looks at the heart and loves us all the time, whether we seem to be doing well or not. So it doesn't matter if you don't get everything sorted straight away. Walk through all issues with an older Christian you trust, and pray and ask God for help - he will deal with everything in you in his perfect timing, as and when he knows you are ready for it. The most important thing is that you want to and are aiming to be like Jesus. *'God began doing a work in you, and I am sure he will continue it until it is finished when Jesus Christ comes again'* (Philippians 1:6).

Jesus was the only person to have walked this earth who was **perfect**

What if I do something wrong again?

Let me tell you now, you will definitely do something wrong again, otherwise you would be perfect - and Jesus was the only person to have walked this earth who was perfect. Your aim should be to live a life that is pleasing to God, but you will make mistakes because you are only human. Forgiveness is not the issue here - Jesus has already forgiven you for ALL your wrong when he died for you on the cross. It is important that we believe this - either the cross has said it all, or the cross has said nothing at all. *'I write to you, dear children, because your sins are forgiven through Christ'* (1 John 2:12). Jesus died once and for all. He didn't just cover your sins and rubbish (that way they would still be there) he took them away completely. The word the Bible uses for this is 'atonement'. If we believe in Jesus and why he came, and have asked him into our lives, we receive the benefit of his forgiveness. *'God loved the world so much that he gave his one and only Son so that whoever believes in him may not be lost, but have eternal life. God did not send his Son into the world to judge the world guilty, but to save the world through him. People who believe in God's Son are not judged guilty. Those who do not believe have already been judged guilty, because they have not believed in God's one and only Son'* (John 3:16-18).

So then, what should you do when you go wrong? Firstly tell God that you are sorry and then ask him to help you not to make the same mistake again. Don't dwell on the fact that you have messed up - God doesn't. Deal with the problem, put it right if possible, and then move on. If it is a problem that keeps happening, find someone you trust to talk through it and help you with it.

● Will I have to stop hanging around with my old mates?

No. God certainly does not want you to abandon your friends when you become a Christian. In fact, he wants you to keep in touch with them so that you have opportunities to tell them about him. You can often be a great example to people who knew you before you were a Christian, because they will see the most change (for the better) in you. However, it is important that you are a good example for your friends and not a bad one. They will be watching your life to see if God really does make a difference. It is therefore important that you do not join in with things that you know are not going to please God or be good for you. If your friends are true friends, you should find that they will respect you for this, although it may be hard for them and you at first if these are things you used to all do together regularly. Why not try introducing your old friends to your new Christian friends and perhaps invite them along to youth group?

There may be some people, though, who it may not be helpful for you to keep hanging around with. If someone consistently makes it too difficult for you to live out your new life with God, and if they keep pulling you back into your old ways, it may mean you need to spend less time with them. Our friends have a huge impact on our lives and we should always choose them carefully. *'Do not change yourselves to be like the people of this world, but be changed within by a new way of thinking. Then you will be able to decide what God wants for you; you will know what is good and pleasing to him and what is perfect'* (Romans 12:2).

Our **friends** have a huge impact on our lives and we should always choose them carefully

● What if my family are not Christians?

Sometimes, if your family are not Christians, it can be difficult for them to cope with the change in you at first. This is because they have known you all your life and know you very well - yet you have made a big decision that may not have had anything to do with them. They may think it is just a phase you are going through, or that you've just gone a bit weird for a while (a member of my family thought I'd been brainwashed!). However, it is important that you are a good example to your parents or guardians by honouring them and doing what they say. The mum of one of my friends actually banned her from going to church and youth group at one point and refused to let her be baptised. Instead of disobeying her, she respected her mum, even though it was difficult - she had to wait about six months and then her mum finally agreed. Once they begin to see the amazing difference

God makes to you, your family will gradually begin to see that you are serious about the decision you have made and may even start showing an interest themselves.

🔵 Can I have a girlfriend/boyfriend who is not a Christian?

There is nothing to stop you from having a friendship with someone who is not a Christian, but having a boyfriend/girlfriend who is not a Christian is not a good idea. The main reason for this is that such relationships hardly ever work without you having to compromise your beliefs at some point. As a Christian, you are going in a different direction to someone who is not a Christian. Picture it this way: having a relationship with a non-Christian is a little bit like you standing on a chair or something else that is raised, and them standing on the floor. If you have ever tried this you will know that it is much easier to be pulled down from the chair than it is to pull the other person up onto the chair with you. As a Christian, I went out with someone who was not a Christian once, and it was one of the most stressful periods of my life. It was horrible not being able to share the most important thing in my life (my friendship with Jesus) with my boyfriend. In the end, I realised that I couldn't please both parties and I had to choose between my boyfriend and God. This decision can determine the course of your whole life, and is not an easy one to make when your emotions are involved. The Bible says this on the subject: *'You are not the same as those who do not believe. So do not join yourselves to them. Good and bad do not belong together. Light and darkness cannot share together. How can Christ and Belial, the devil, have any agreement? What can a believer have together with a non-believer?'* (2 Corinthians 6:14-15).

it is much

easier to be

pulled down

than it is to

pull the

other person up

What if I get picked on or lose friends because I've become a Christian?

Not everybody will understand why you have become a Christian and this may bring some difficulties for you. People these days are not used to others having strong and definite beliefs, and they can feel threatened by someone who has different beliefs to them. However, a bully will bully someone for any reason at all - whether you are wearing the right trainers, or have a trendy enough haircut etc. Being a Christian is just something else they can pick on. Bullies are weak people who pick on something different in someone else, just to make them feel bigger and better. Although this can be tough to face, their opinions are worth nothing. If you are convinced of what you believe and are not embarrassed about it, they will soon get bored of picking on you. As for friends, if they do not respect your beliefs and the decision you have made, are they worth having as friends in the first place? I found with many of my friends that once they knew I was a Christian they thought it was cool that you could be a Christian and still have fun and a laugh, even though they could see I was trying to do the right things. They would also end up coming to me to talk if they had any problems and would even ask me to pray about things for them!

they would even ask me to pray about things for them!

Do I have to go to Church every Sunday?

You do not have to go to church every single Sunday, but hopefully, as you get to know God better, you will want to go as often as you can. Church is not supposed to be a boring chore that you attend out of obligation, it is meant to be a place where you can go and enjoy learning more about Jesus and worship God, while meeting with other Christians. There are easy

57

and harder things about Church, as with most things, but it is all good for your growth as a Christian. It is a bit like the food we eat - it is easy to eat chips and ice-cream and other yummy stuff, but when it comes to sprouts and liver (yuck!) that's a different matter. However, a balanced diet is essential if we are to be healthy. To make it easier for you, make sure that the Church you go to loves Jesus and teaches the Bible and has a good youth group with people your own age.

If God is there, then why do bad things happen?

Most of us have wondered about this question at some point or other - and if you haven't, then you may well be asked it by one of your friends - as it is something many people don't understand. Sometimes, when we look at the world, or turn on the TV and watch the news, we can wonder where God is in the midst of the mess. There is so much crime, violence and hatred in the world today. It is easy for us to point the finger at God and blame him. However, God hates all the bad stuff that goes on, and his heart breaks for us when he sees us suffering. The thing is, God made us with the fantastic gift of 'free will'. This means we have the freedom to choose to be as bad as we want or as good as we want. Unfortunately, a lot of the bad in the world is down to human beings choosing to do wrong. Sometimes people even cause suffering and say it is in the name of Jesus, when of course it has nothing to do with him.

When it comes to sickness and natural disasters it is difficult to find an answer that comforts us. But we have to remember that things in the world got messed up when mankind first decided to rebel against God and started to sin (do wrong). In the beginning, the world was perfect - it had none of these problems - just as we have the freedom to **choose** to be as **bad** as we want or as **good** as we want

God intended it to be. When mankind went their own way, things got turned upside down. This is why there are unexplainable things happening all the time. Although it can seem unfair that God allows these things to happen, we know that he does not cause them. However, one day he will return and put everything right!

If God made us, who made God?

This is a hard question to get your head around, but no one actually made God. God has always been there and always will be. In the Bible it says, 'In the beginning God created the sky and the earth' (Genesis 1:1). God is the creator and we are the created. If something or someone had created God then he wouldn't be God - they would. Every thing starts and finishes with God. He is outside of time and all-powerful, so nobody made him.

How do you know that God is real?

Although we cannot see God, it does not mean that he does not exist. There are lots of things that we can't see which we know are real. For example, we can't see electricity, but we know that it's there because we can see the effects of it when we turn on an electrical appliance. It is the same with God: although we cannot see him we can see and feel the effects of him being in our lives. Our experience of him shows us that he is there and real. Furthermore, I think we only have to look around at the wonderful things in the world to see signs of God everywhere. Sometimes it may feel as if God is not there or that he is not listening to what you are saying, but just because you can't always 'feel' him there, it does not mean he isn't there. At times like this, try to remember how you felt when you first became a Christian and what made you want to make that decision.

● If God is good, then why does he send people to hell?

The whole issue of heaven and hell is that it really comes down to the decisions we make while we are alive here on Earth. God does not force us to do anything - we have free will. Jesus actually spoke more about heaven than he did about hell. This was because he didn't want anyone to go there. The reason God sent Jesus was to give everyone the opportunity to accept him and to find their way to heaven through him. However, if someone goes through their whole life here saying 'God I don't want to know you, I don't want you to have anything to do with my life', then God will underline the decision that they have made when their life ends. Heaven is basically eternity with God, which means everything good, and will be more wonderful than we can begin to imagine. Hell is eternity without God - the reality of this will actually be a lot worse than we can imagine.

if someone goes through their whole life here saying 'God I don't want to know you, I don't want you to have anything to do with my life', then God will underline the **decision** that they have made when their life ends.

● What if I have doubts about the decision I've made to be a Christian?

As I have said all along in this book, it is OK to have doubts and questions, and you will have them. The question is, what to do with them when they do come up. It is important not to keep them to yourself. If you do, they will build up until you have steam coming out of your ears and you'll end up giving up. Instead . . .

* Find someone to talk to. They may not be able to answer all your questions, but they can certainly try, and it helps so much to get it all out in the open. The chances are that they have had the same doubts and questions themselves at some point in their lives. This will help you to realise that you are not the only one.

* Be honest. Be truthful about how you feel, even if you feel bad for feeling that way. It's OK to be totally honest about what's going on in your head - it is the first step to being closer to an answer.

* Ask God. God is knows everything - he knows how you are feeling and wants to help you find a satisfying answer. Sometimes there won't be an answer for us to understand, because God's ways are often different to ours and we will never understand everything while we are here on earth. But God can give us peace so that we no longer worry about it anyway.

* Don't worry. Having doubts and questions is all part of growing up as a Christian. It is a good sign that we want to know why we believe what we believe. Not only does this help us to answer other people's questions in the future, but it also gives us a good base for a lasting faith through good times and bad times.

'God has given me a **joy** inside so that, no matter what bad things happen to me, **I know God is with me** and will get me through the situation, if I just **turn to him and ask for help.** I don't feel lost any more. For a long time I felt lost and didn't have a purpose and **now I've got that purpose – to please God.**'

– David

The truth is, it is not always easy to be a Christian, but it is more than worth it. Jesus said, 'Enter through the narrow gate. The gate is wide and the road is wide [easy] that leads to hell, and many people enter through that gate. But the gate is small and the road is narrow [hard] that leads to true life. Only few people find that road' (Matthew 7:13-14).

WORDS FROM THE SHINE GIRLS:

'**Most people have questions and doubts about their faith,** especially when they are first getting to know God. The only time that this is a problem is when the doubts are not talked about. **God is not threatened or intimidated by our doubts and questions.** Asking questions and confronting doubts make your **faith deeper** and more secure in the end.'

– Nic

10 first steps for the new Christian

① **Make sure you are a Christian** - have you prayed the prayer?

② **Tell someone**

③ **Set a regular time to spend with God** - get alone with God and read the Bible

④ **Pray** - *See Chapter 3*

⑤ **Make Christian friends**

⑥ **Find a church & youth group that suit you**

⑦ **Find an 'accountability' friend** - a Christian you look up to

⑧ **Get baptised** - this is only for when you feel ready. Baptism is when you get completely submerged (dunked) under water. It symbolises leaving your old life behind as you come up from the water. It is a declaration of your faith and a display of commitment to God.

⑨ **Memorise God's words**

⑩ **Ask for help when you're struggling**

In conclusion, I just want to encourage you to go for it and not look back. You can make a whole world of difference! *'As you have received Christ Jesus the Lord, so continue to live in him. Keep your roots deep in him and have your lives built on him. Be strong in the faith just as you were taught, and always be thankful'* (Colossians 2:6-7). And I have some great advice for you, especially for young people, straight from God's word: *'Do not let anyone treat you as unimportant because you are young. Instead, be an example to the believers with your words, your actions, your love, your faith, and your pure life'* (1 Timothy 4:12).

WORDS FROM THE SHINE GIRLS:

'Don't be lukewarm. If you do you will have such a miserable life. The most boring people I know are lukewarm Christians – neither hot nor cold. Love God with all your heart – that's what he wants – he wants your heart. I promise you, life is exciting when you live it HOT for God!'

– Hanne

GO FOR IT!